Hollywood in Color

NANDY DEL CASTILLO

Copyright © 2021 Nandy Del Castillo
All rights reserved.
ISBN: 9798527941432

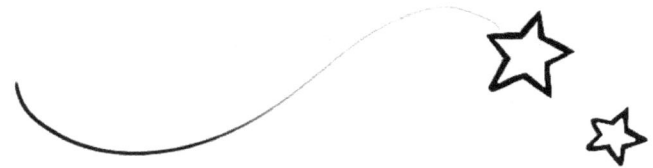

This book is dedicated to all the dreamers.
Silence every voice of doubt and
continue to push through.

Believe that it is possible,

To Megan, Ana, and Alex for making
a dreamer a doer.

"What excites me the most is that I have been able to be involved in projects that will be used as history lessons — stories of real life people who made larger-than-life sacrifices. Stories that spark conversations between us all and make us challenge the things we know to be unjust.

-Algee Smith

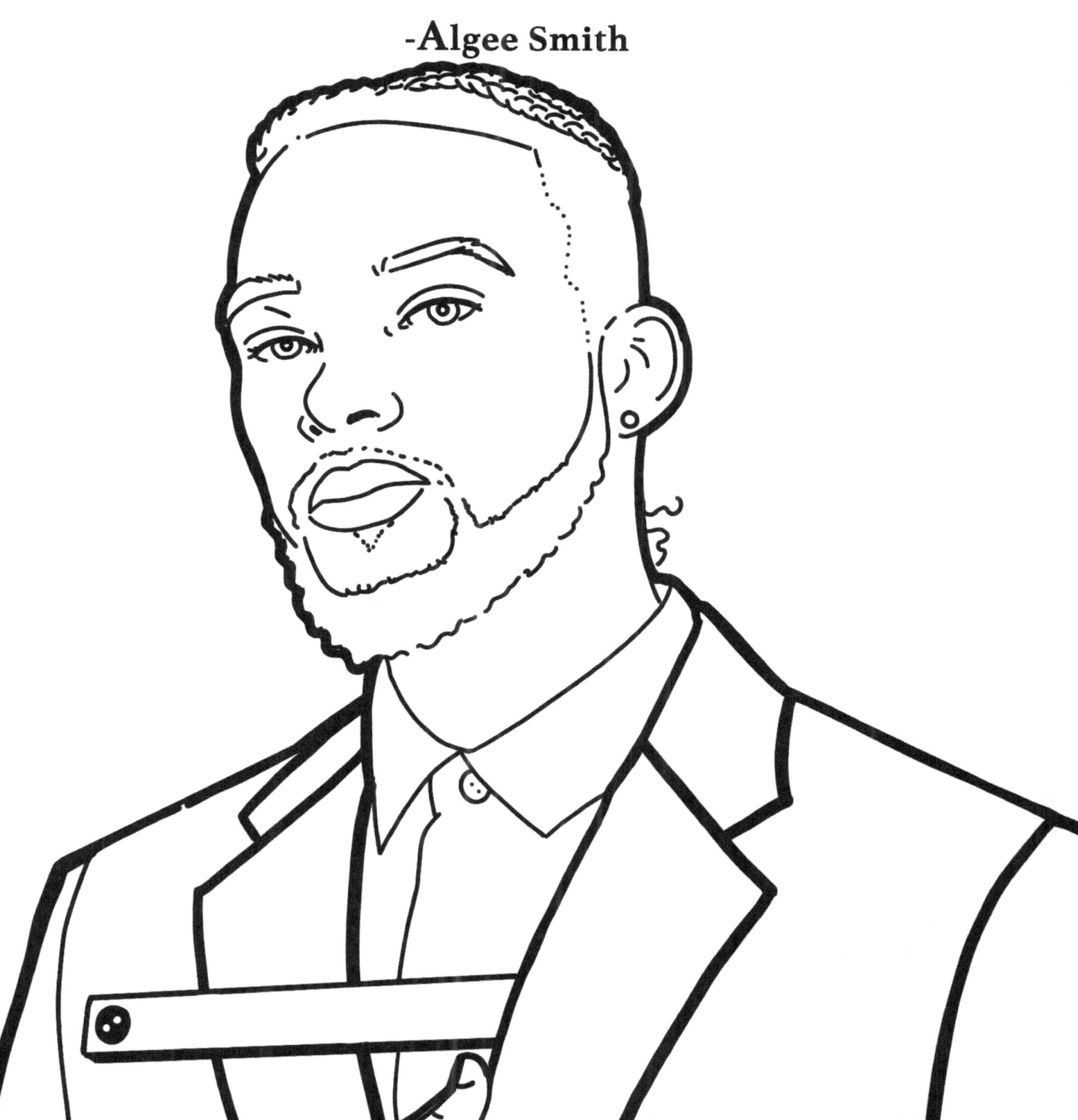

"I don't have to prove anything to anyone, I only have to follow my heart and concentrate on what I want to say to the world. I run my world."

-Beyoncé

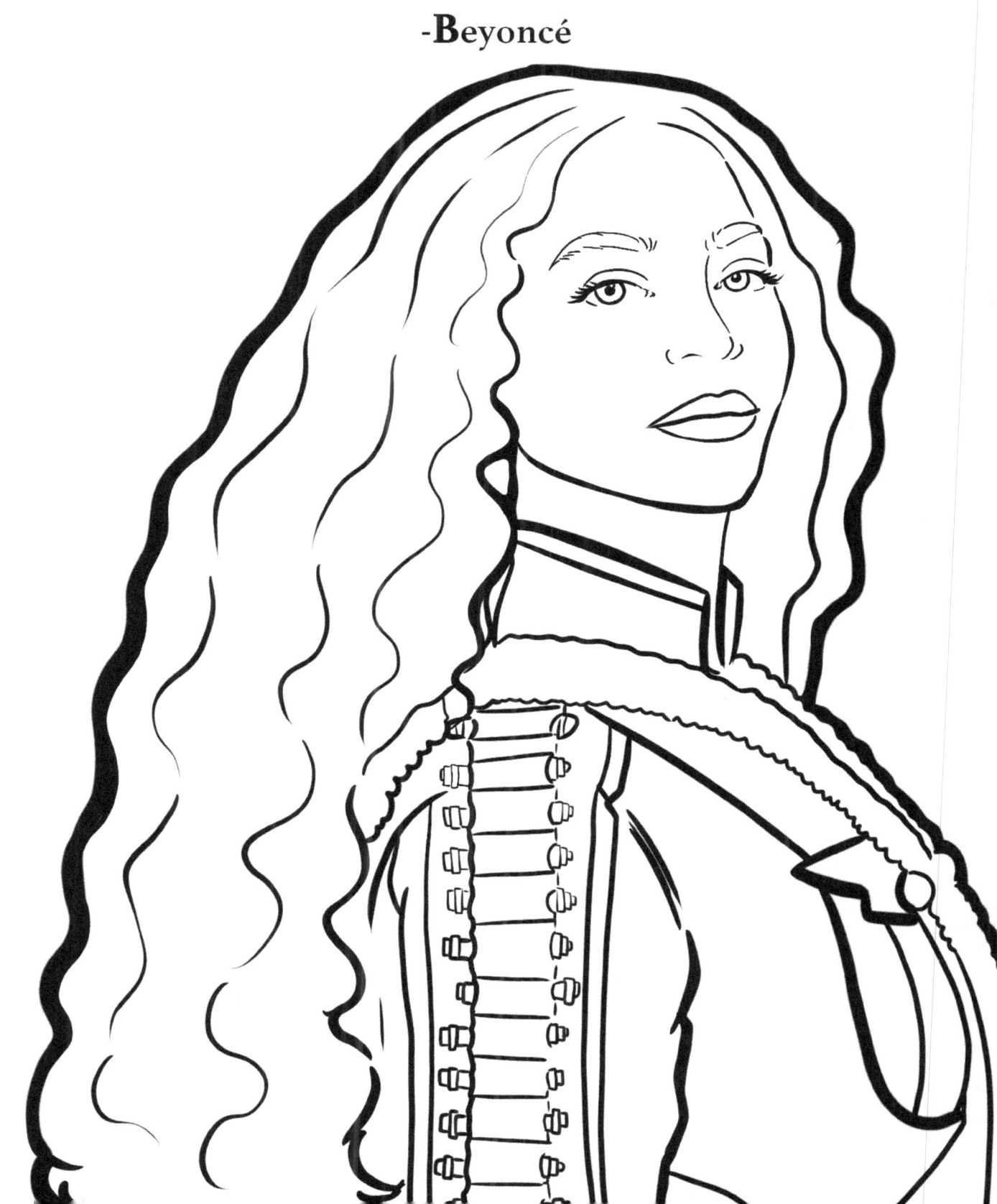

"If you see the world unbalanced, be a crusader that pushes heavily on the seesaw of the mind."

- Chadwick Boseman

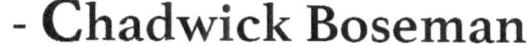

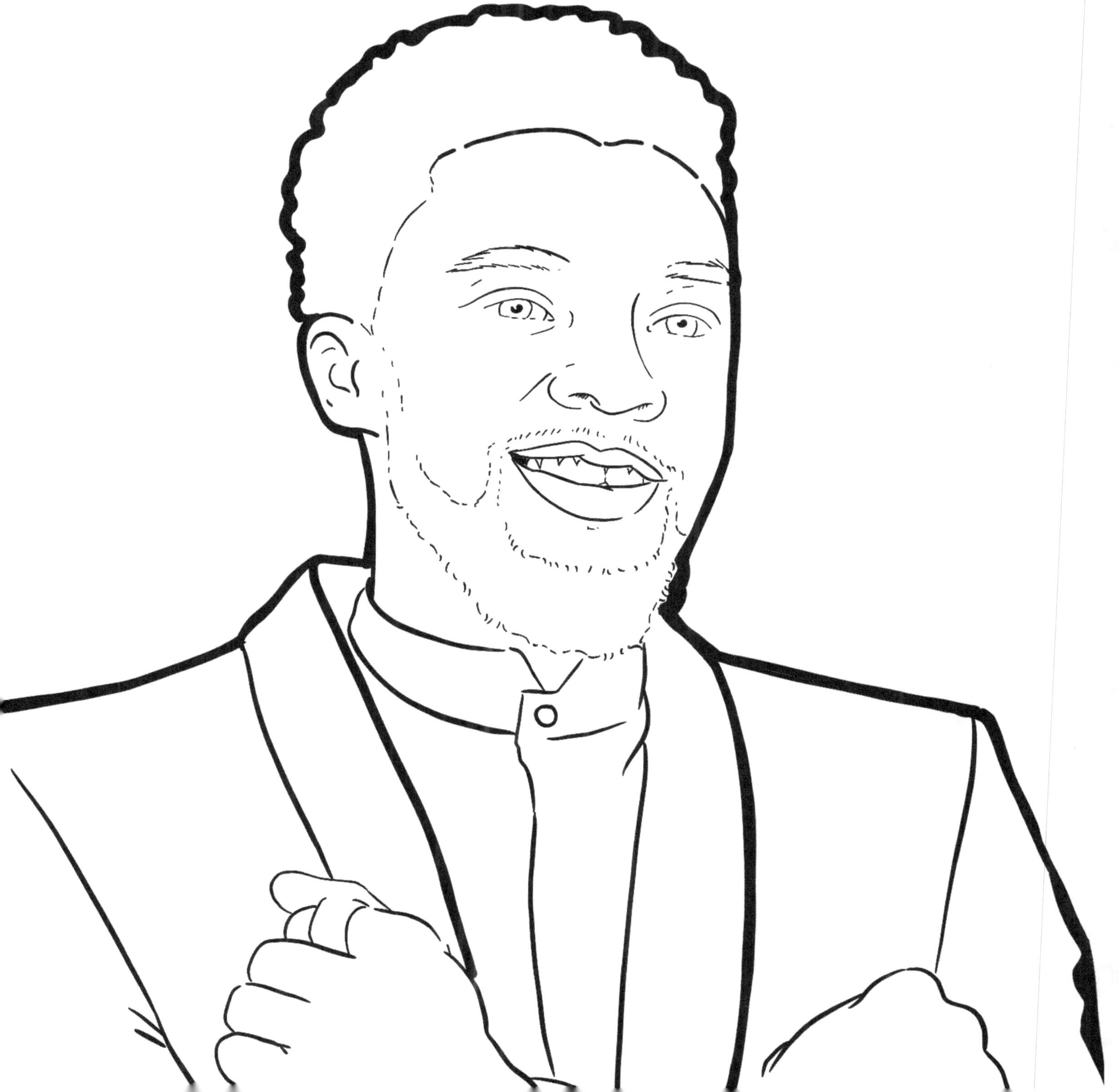

"I'm not scared of the future at all. The future is progress if you treat it right."

-Donald Glover Jr. (Childish Gambino)

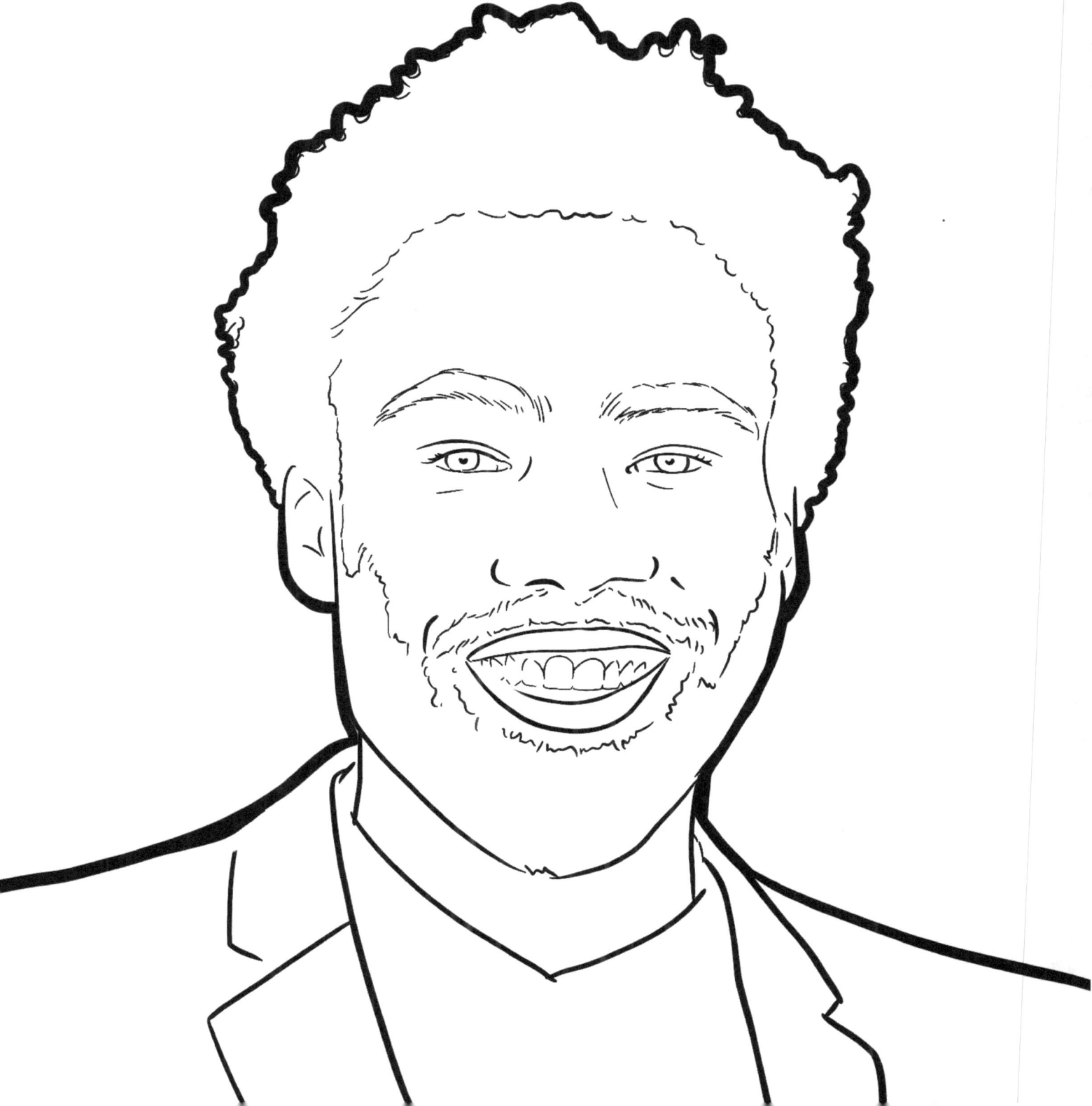

"Guess I was born to make mistakes but I ain't scared to take the weight so when I stumble off the path I know my heart will guide me back."

-Erykah Badu

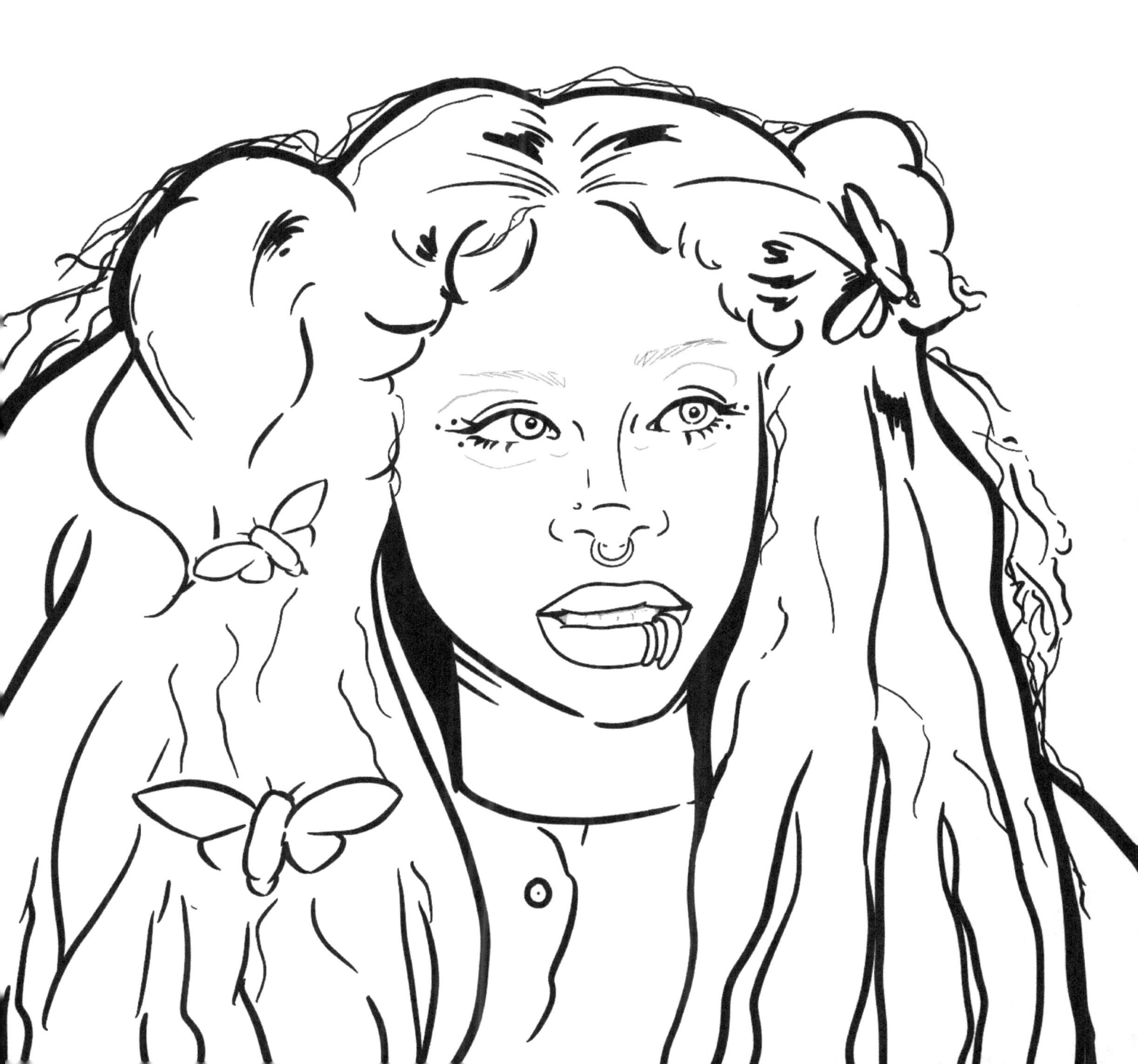

"Hate it or love it the underdog's on top and I'm gon' shine homie until my heart stop..."

-Fifty Cent

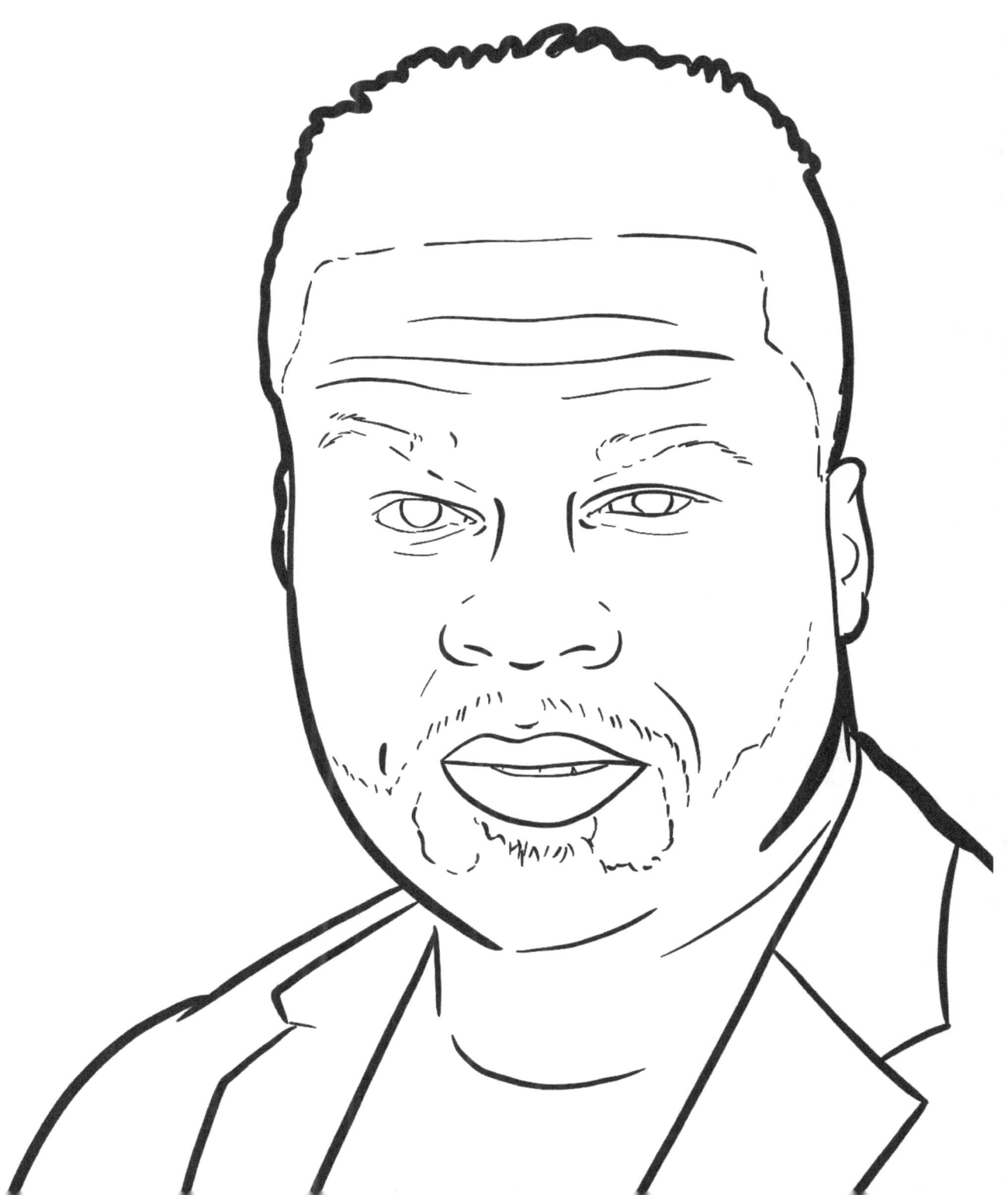

"Don't worry about society's conditioning and the labels that are put on you by external forces. Hold onto your true self."
- Gugu Mbatha-Raw

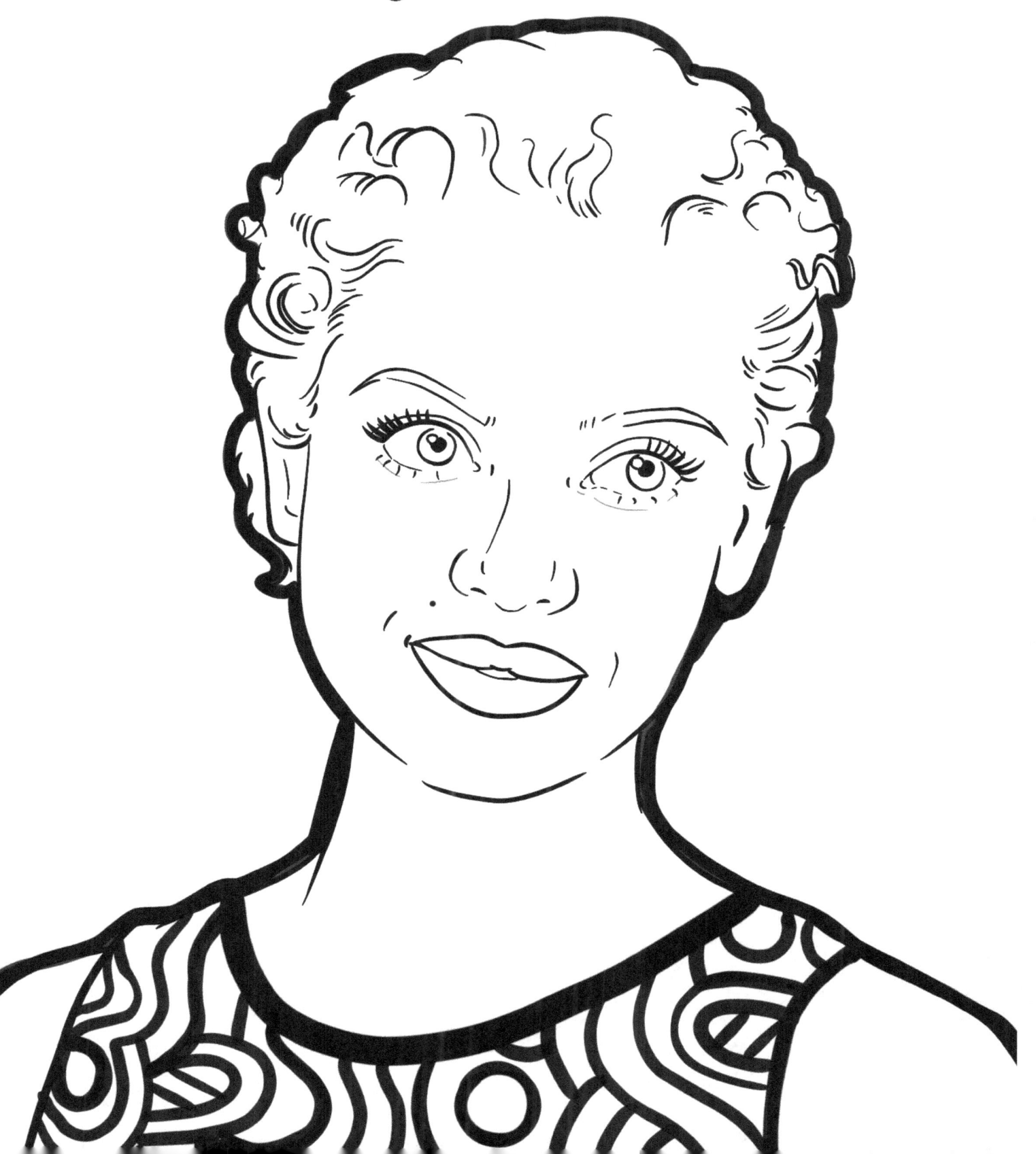

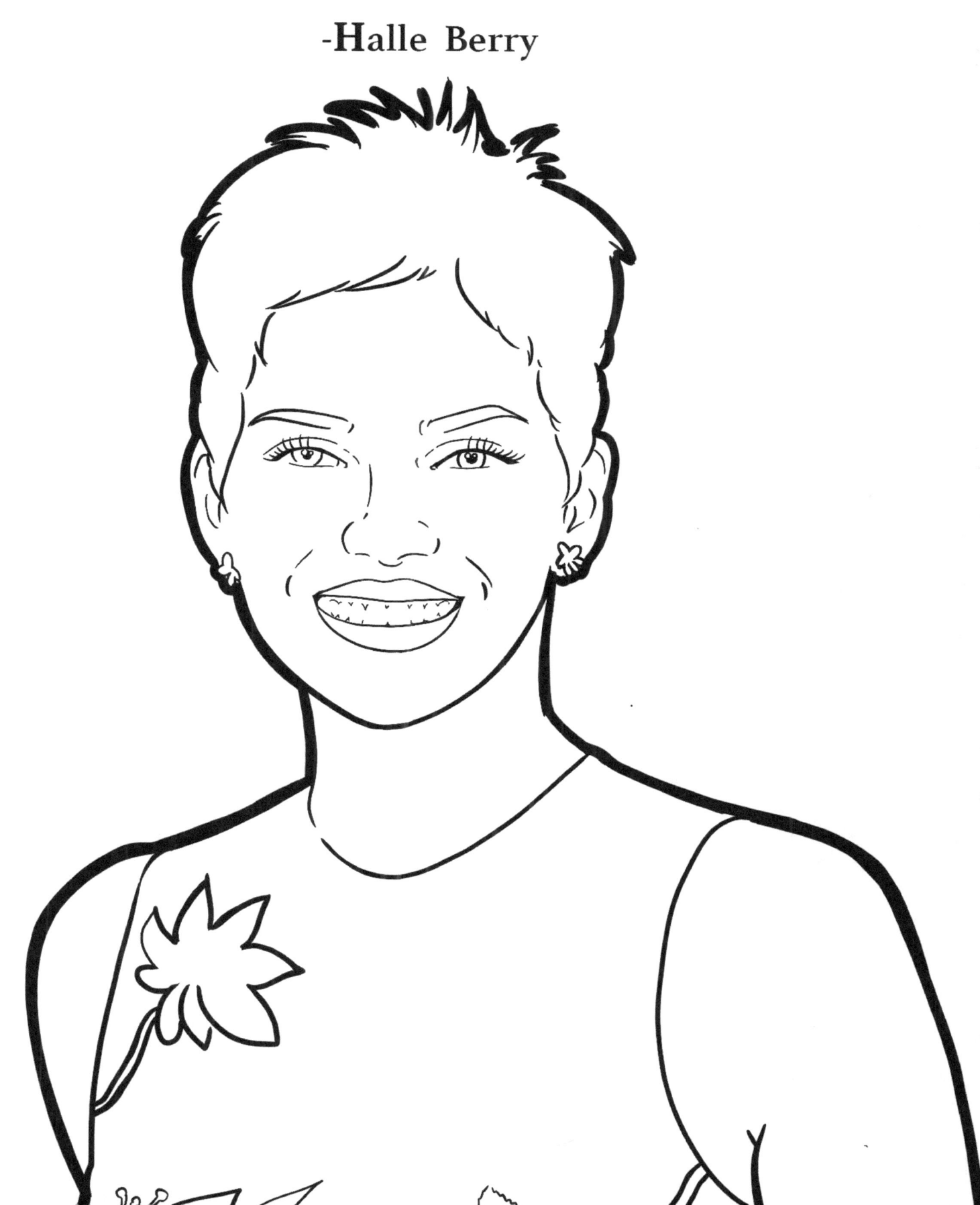
"Humor is always part of the best hours in life."

-Halle Berry

"For a long time, much like Yara said, I defined myself by what I wasn't, which constantly set me up for failure and disappointment." And, my life changed when I focused on what I was good at, what I liked most about myself and what made me stand out."
- Issae Rae

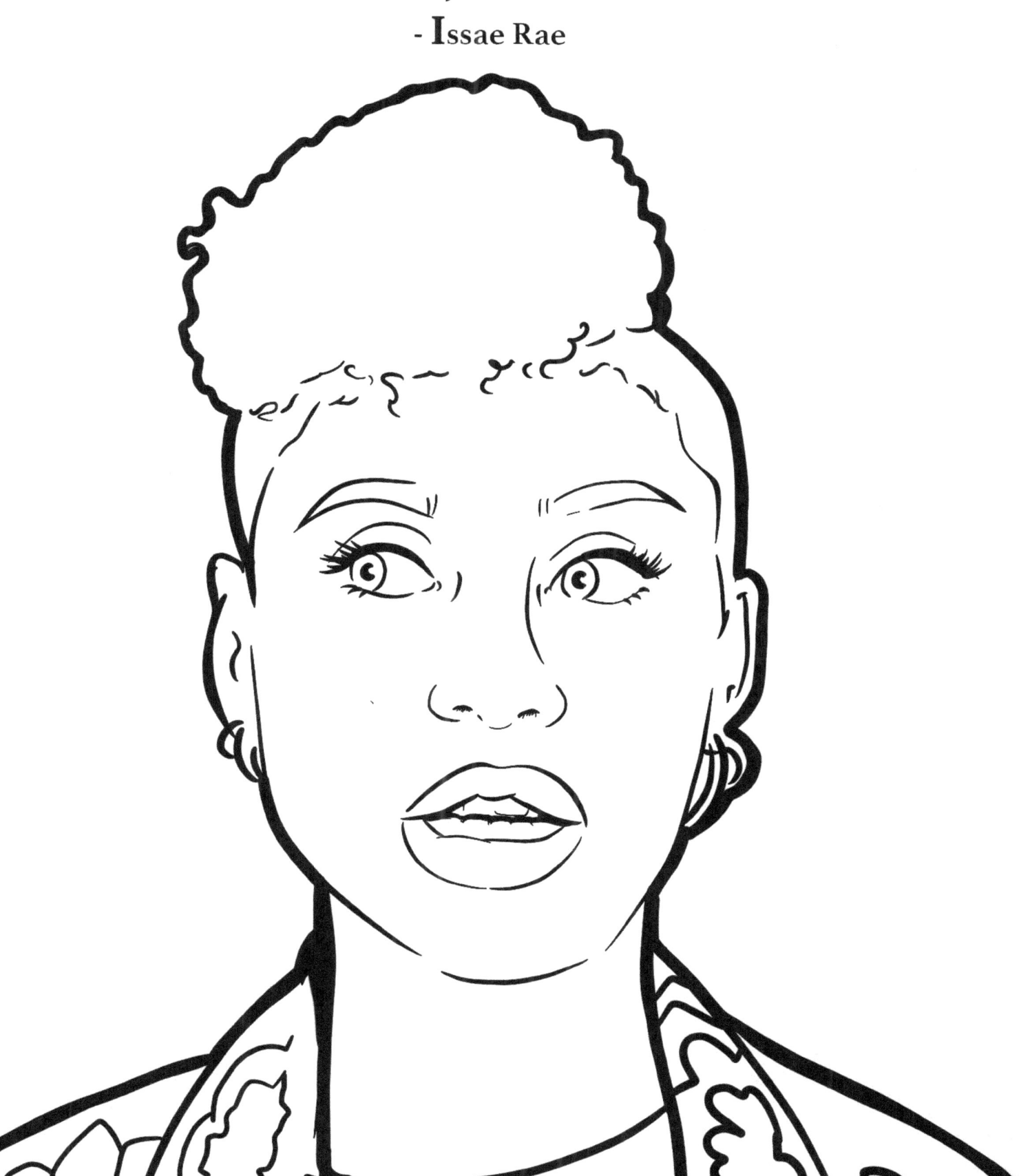

" Let's get used to other cultures. Portray the world for what it is and you will find truth."

-John Boyega

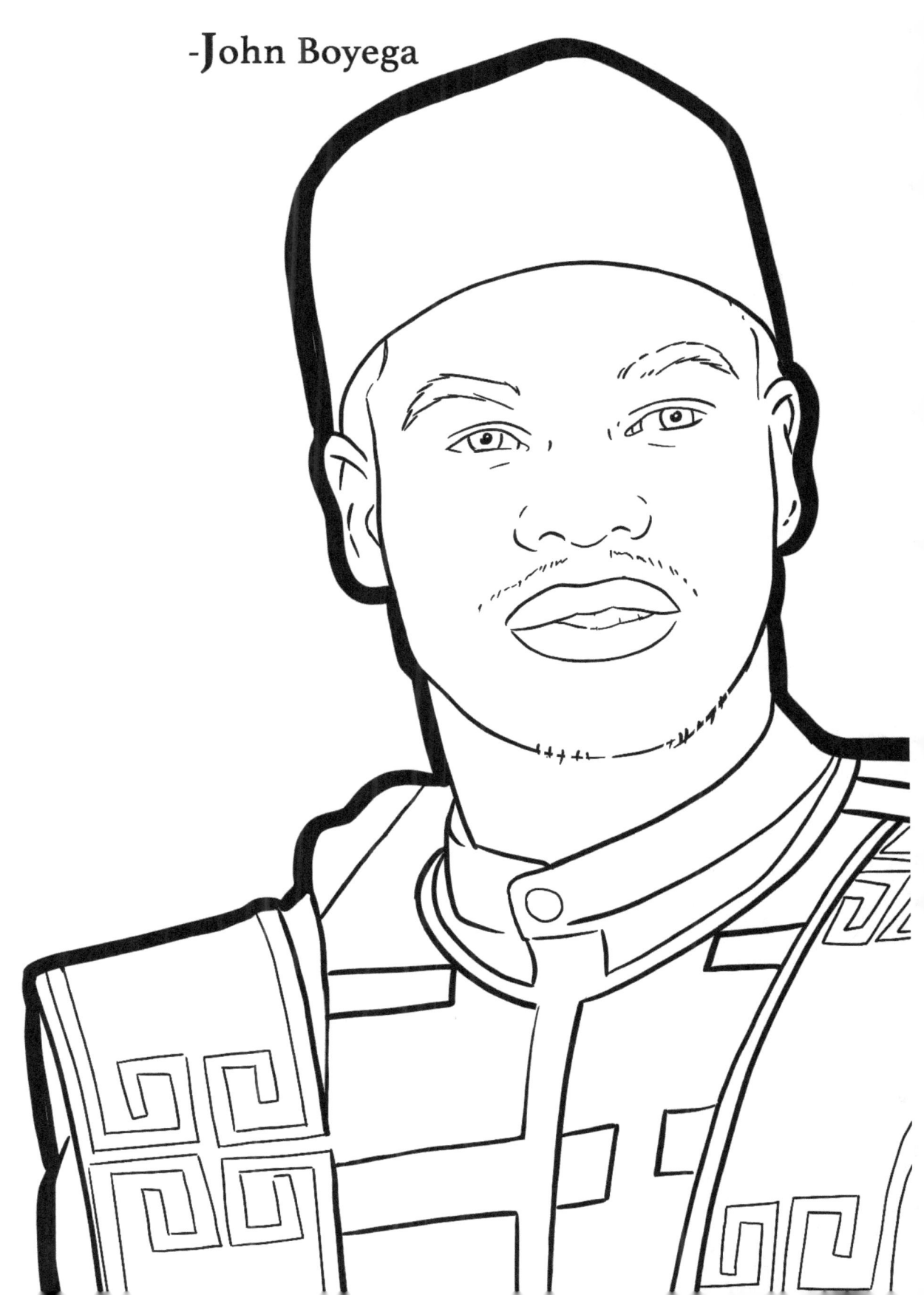

Follow your heart's truth with no need for personal gain other than the feeling produced when doing what you truly love
-Keke Palmer

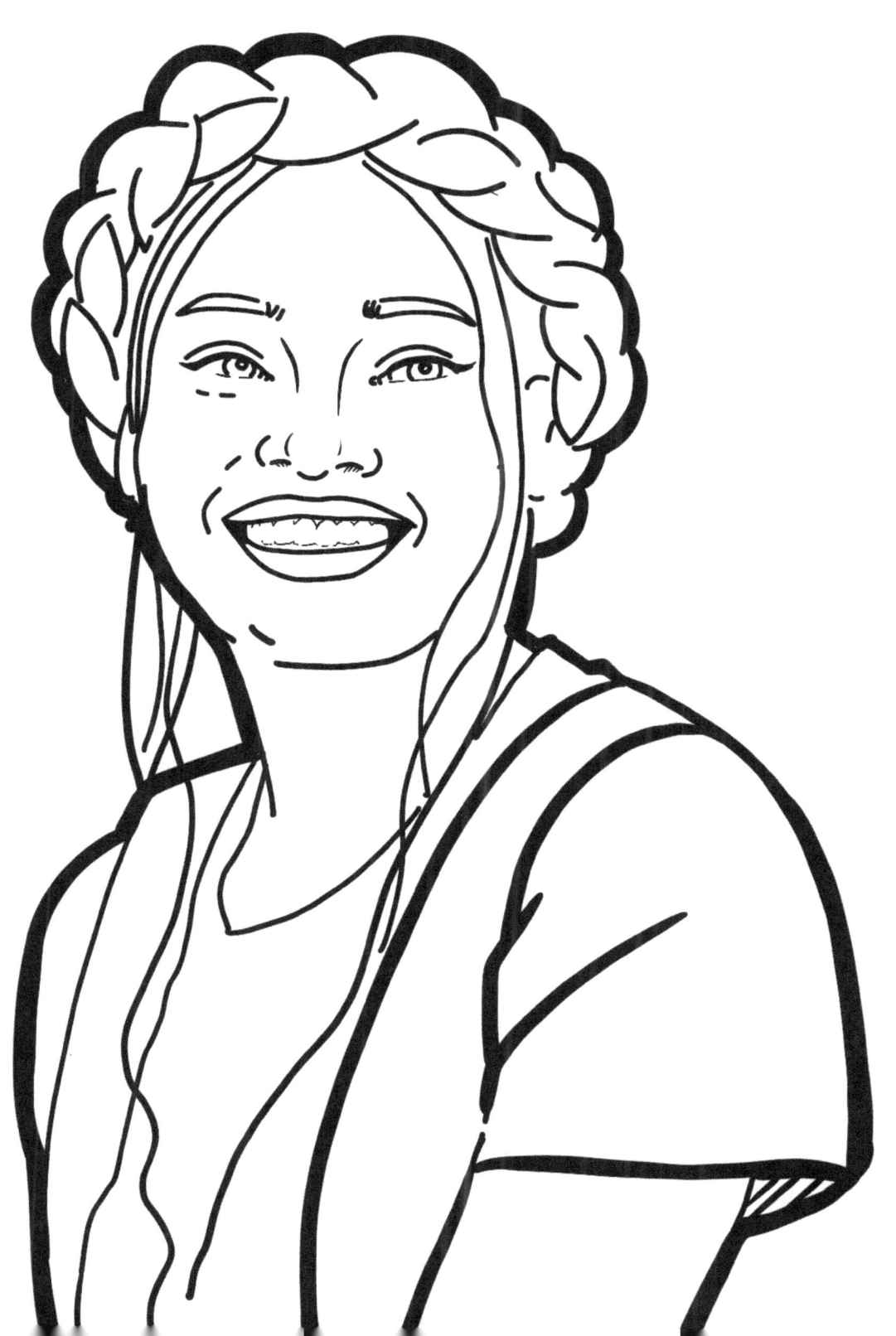

"I don't think [Alexander Hamilton and Aaron Burr] are great parenting examples." Hamilton serves as a great warning about what not to do, but if you freeze things in time, looking at just that moment of those two young parents — with Hamilton looking over Philip's cradle and Burr looking over Theodosia's cradle — the promise that they make to those kids to be the best version of themselves, to pave the way and make sure that the road is a kinder and righter way than they walked, that's what we cling to as parents."

-Leslie Odom Jr.

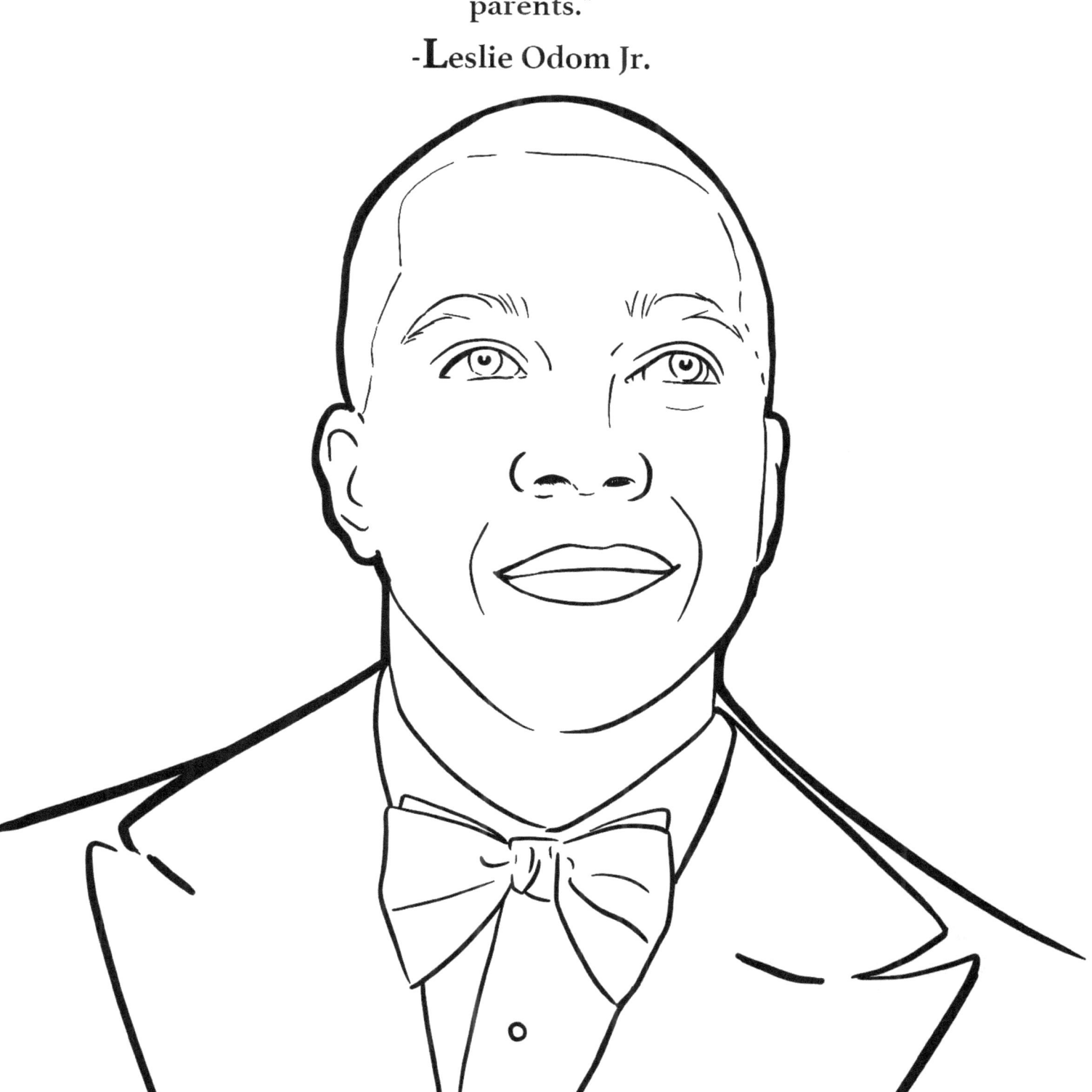

As human beings, why does it take somebody to feel like they're close to us for us to see their humanity? Why can't we see the humanity in people that are distant from us?

-Michael B Jordan

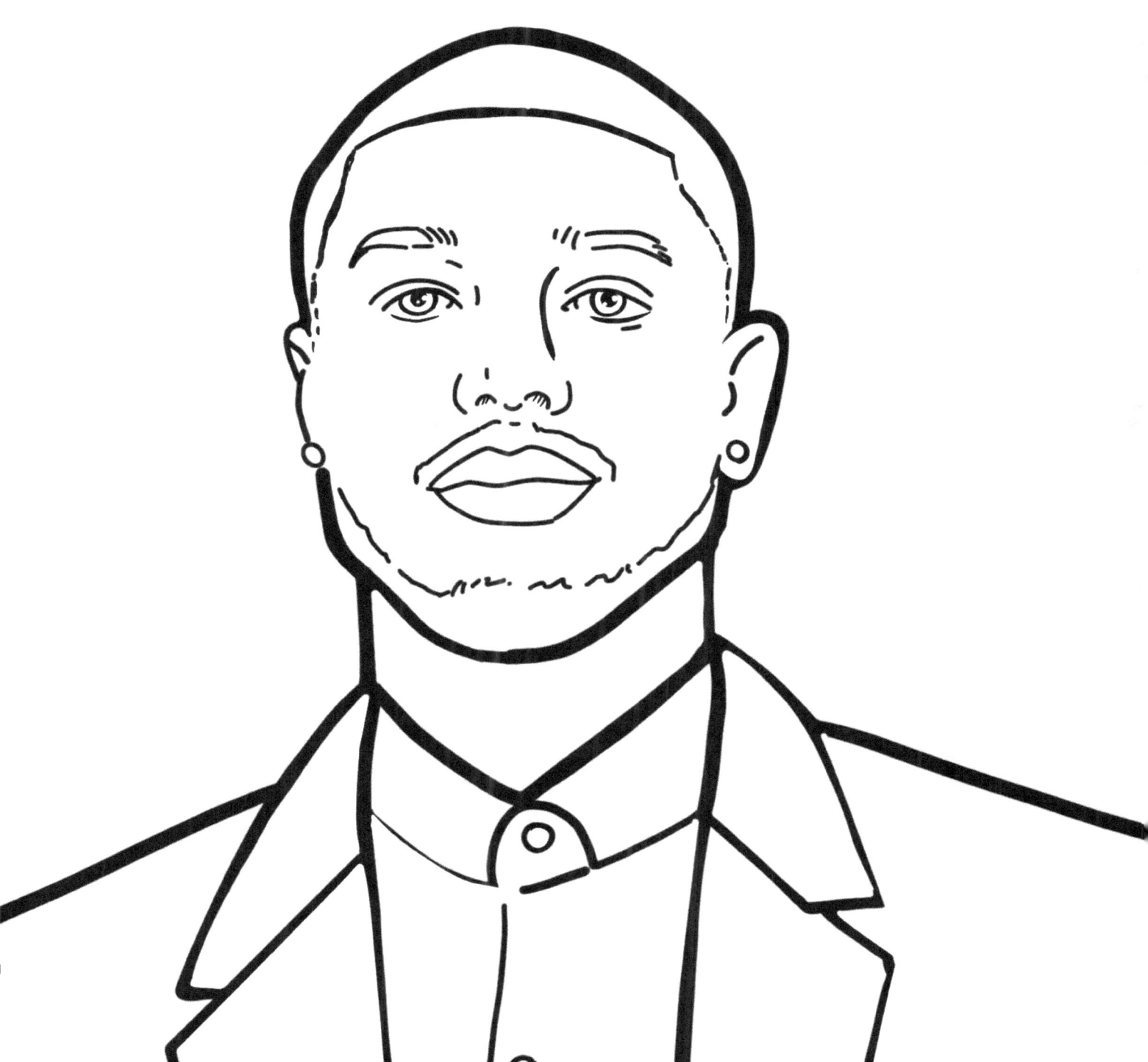

"On a personal level, because of the impact that Fast & Furious has had for me as a woman of mixed Black heritage, and seeing the diversity of those movies and how they grow, being a part of that huge impact that those movies have across the entire world was just so exciting. The idea that someone might one day see me and feel represented the way that I did when I was a kid."

-Nathalie Emmanuel

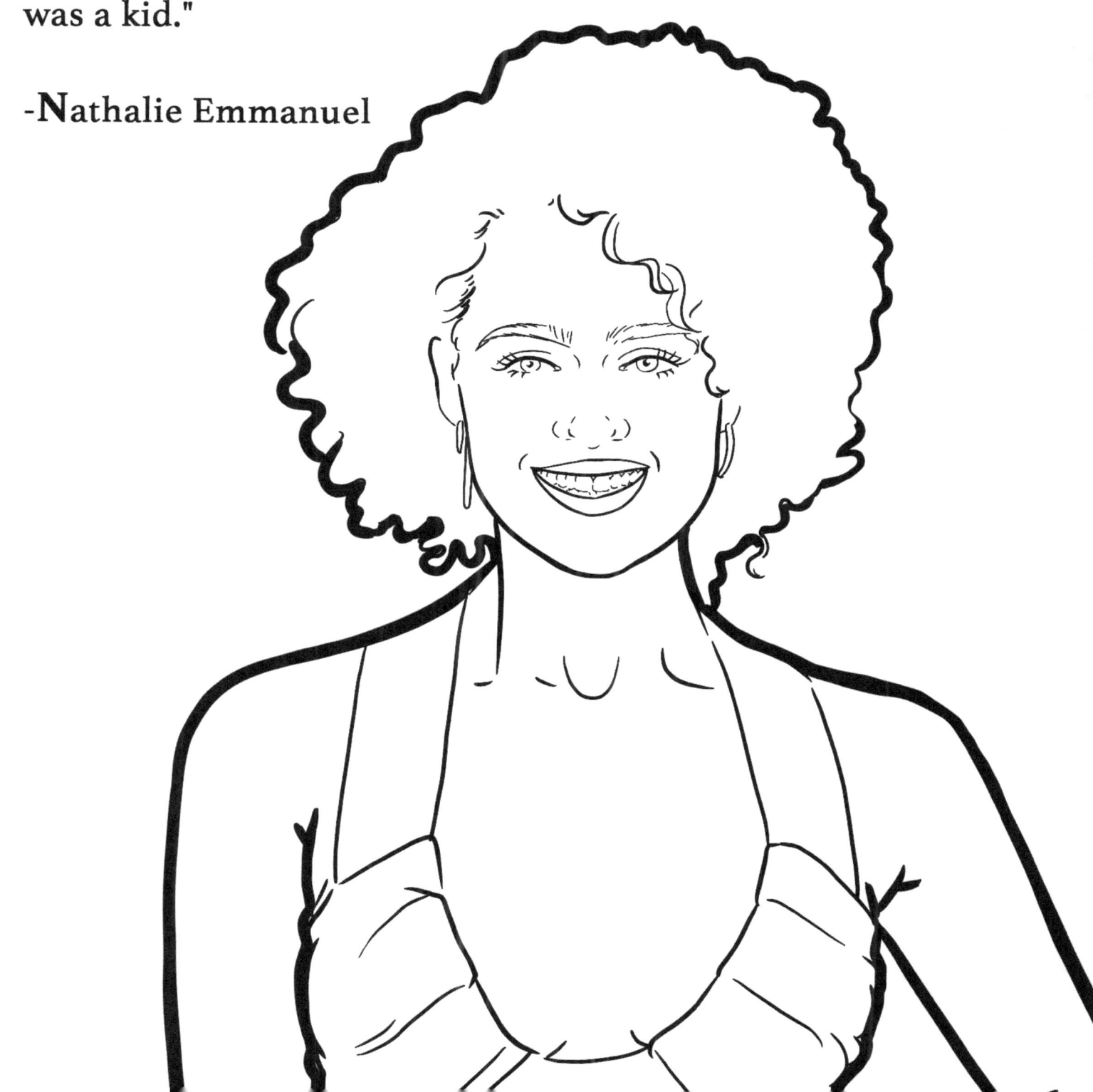

"I walked in thinking, "I have ten movies under my belt and now they want me to go back to making commercials?" I said, if I do that, I want it to be funny. Quite honestly, I didn't think the deal was going to make, because I wanted part of the creative control. I was impressed that they were making an offer to a non-athlete young black male to be a spokesperson for two and a half years. To their credit, they said, absolutely yes, they never questioned anything I wanted to do. It was a blessed experience for me."
- Orlando Jones

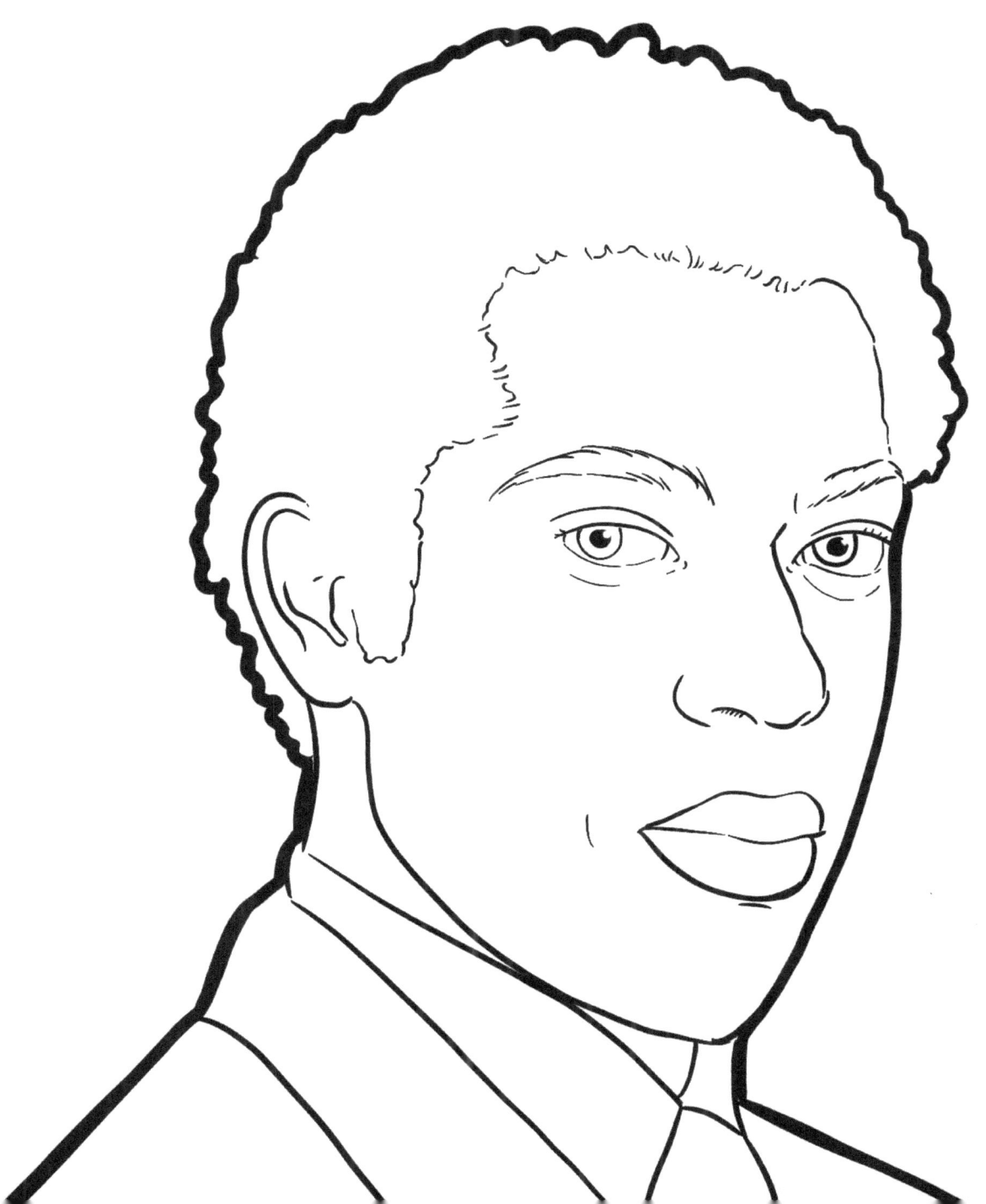

"When people wouldn't see me for a role, it was a recognition of the power of the beauty in women, of something that's so captivating it can be distracting against the work.

-Pam Gier

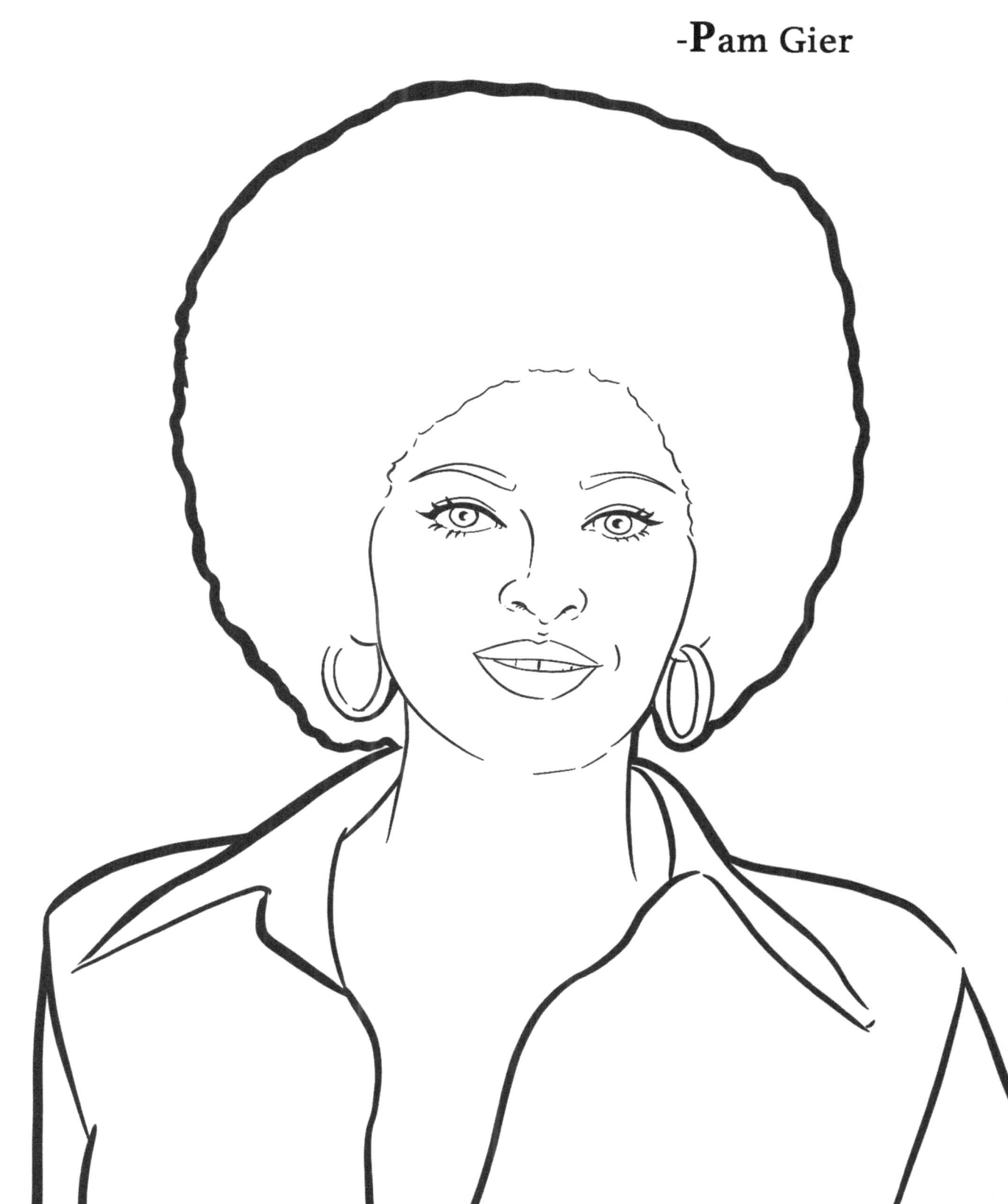

"That's what I like about Annie. If she has goals, she'll finish them, like me. We're both confident."

-Quvenzhane Wallis

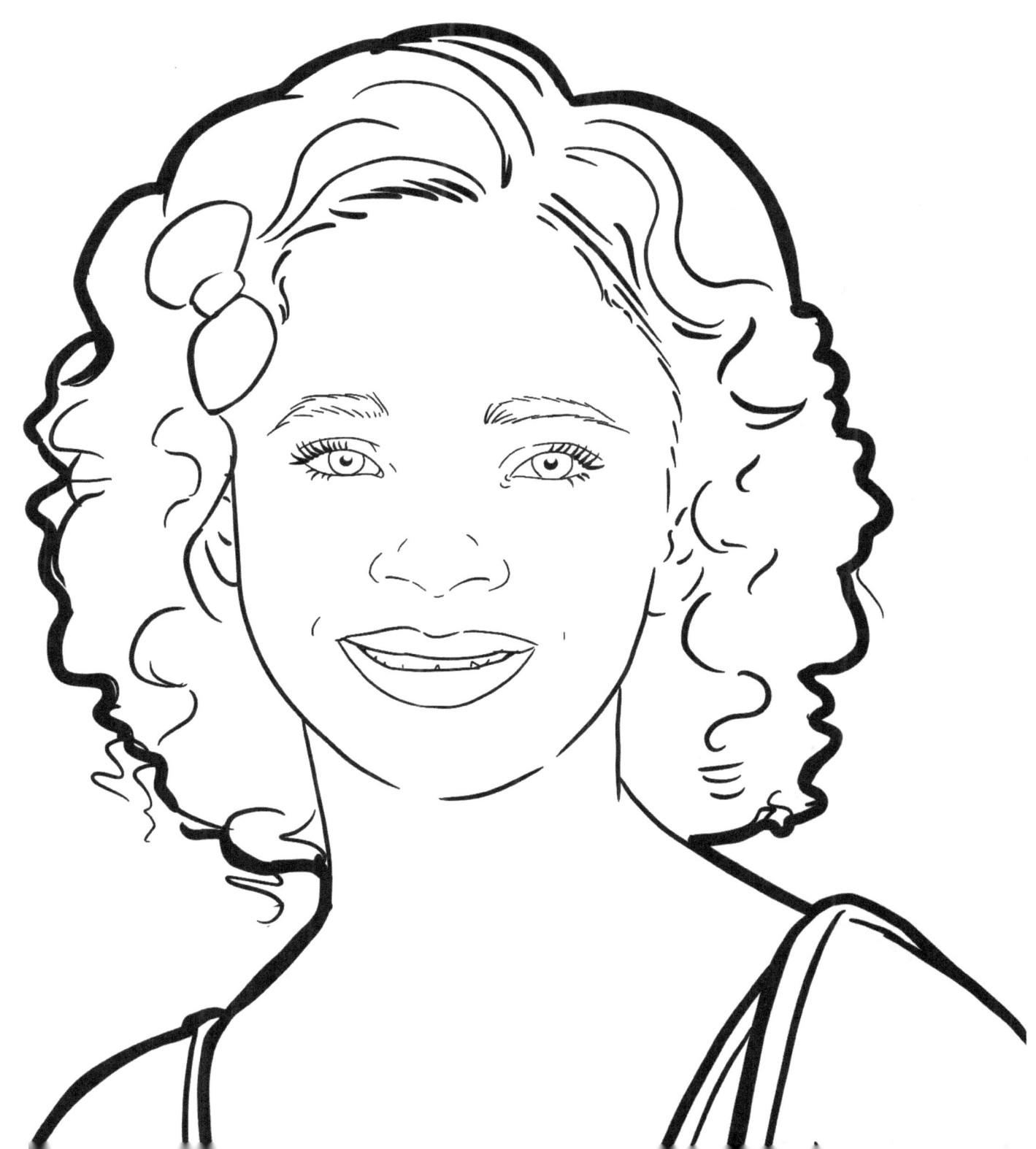

"There's a new Mozart, a new Miles Davis, a new Misty Copeland, a new Matisse potentially languishing in a math class somewhere. If we fail to introduce them to art, we fail humanity."

-Renee Elis Goldberry

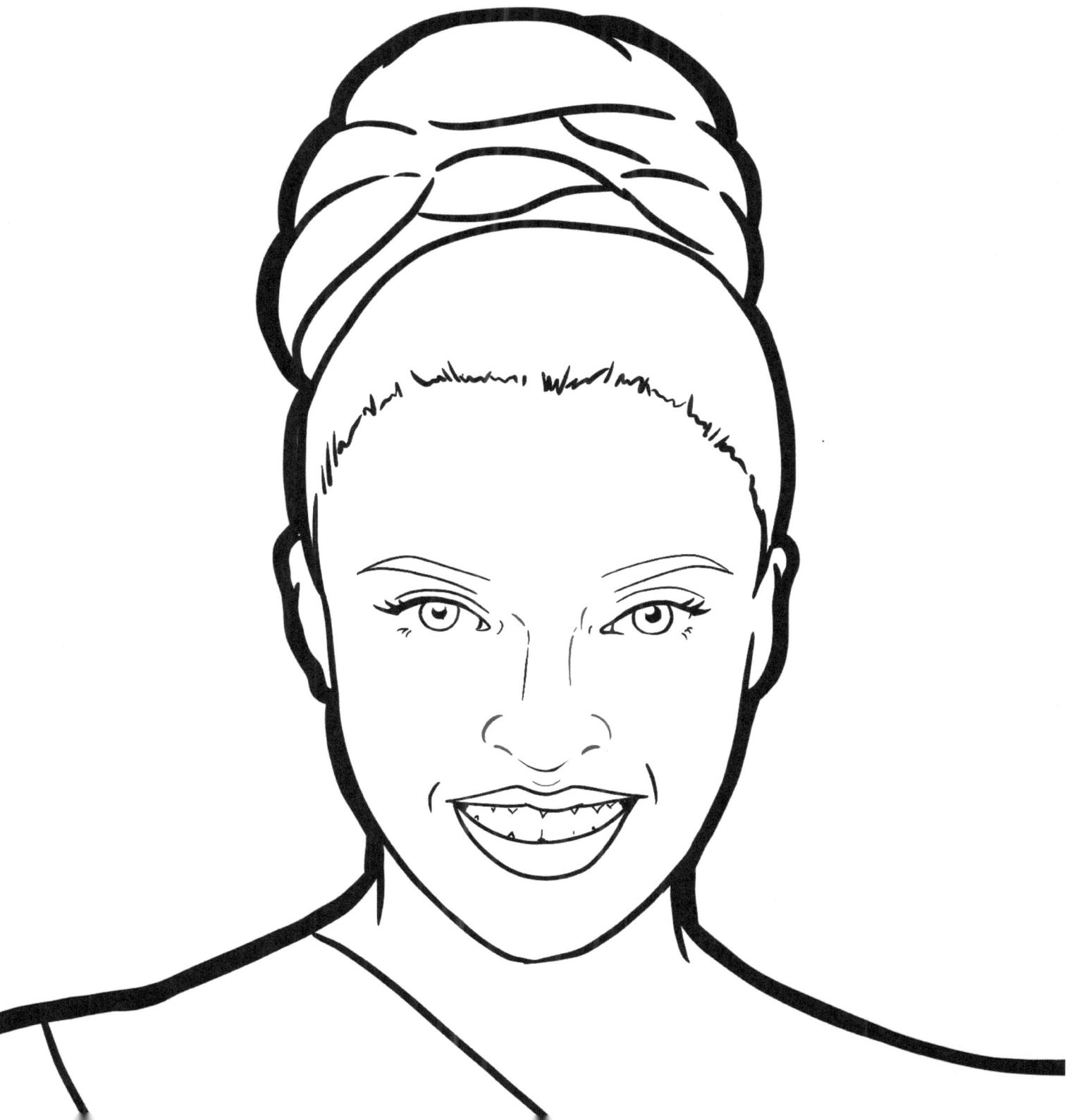

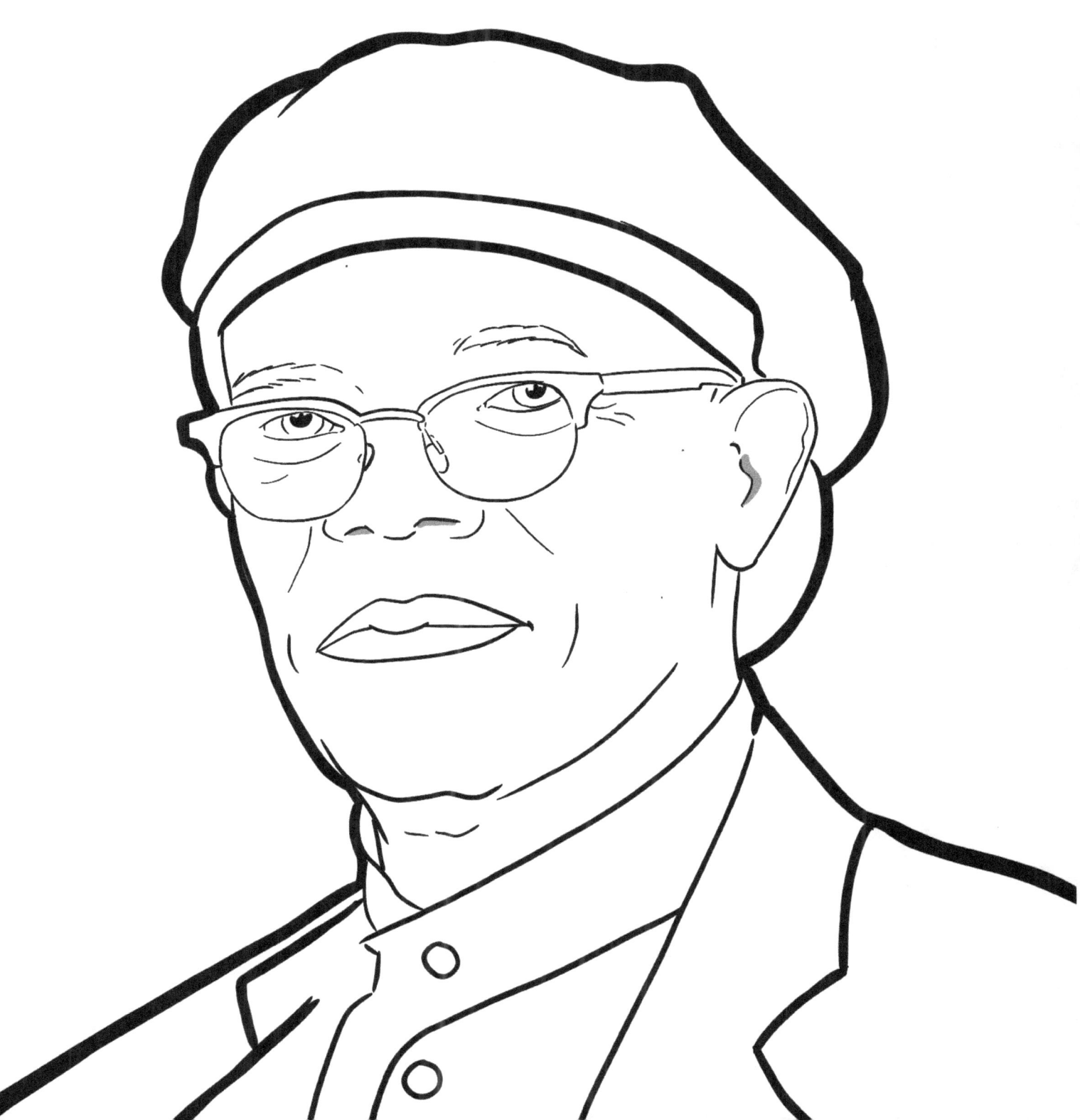

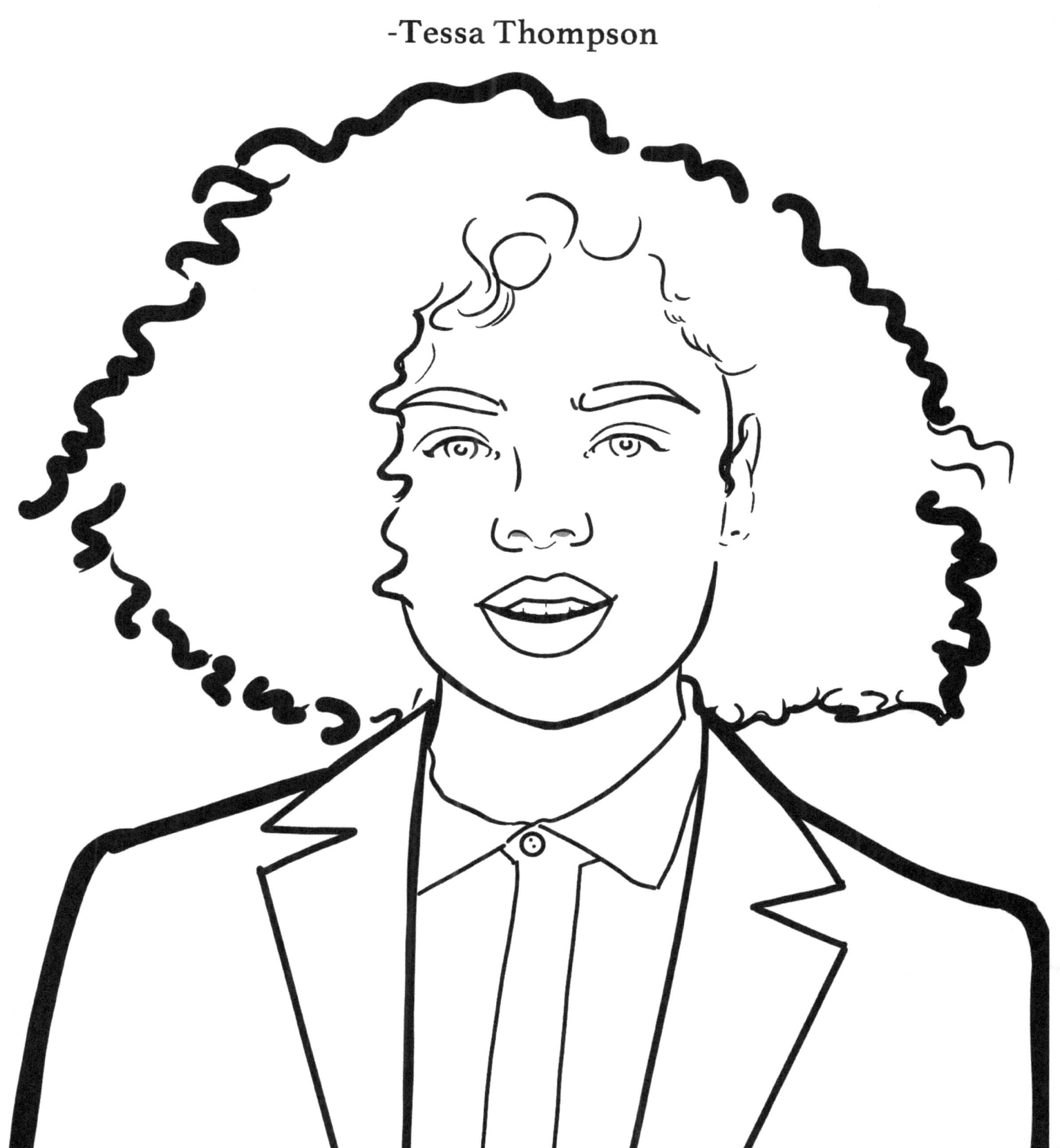

"Yeah, I think it is an actor's dream. For me, regardless of what medium you working in, whether I'm on a stage or on a big screen or small, I feel like the work is always the same, we're trying to get to something that's human at its core and honest and truthful."

-Tessa Thompson

I think women should pursue and attack whatever it is that satisfies them in their life. Also, I'd tell women that you must bet on you. If you want to make your passion your work, then you must be prepared to work hard on your passion. Forget about if no one else can bet on you, forget about if nobody believes. If you believe, that is the only thing you need to carry in your soul."

- Uzo Aduba

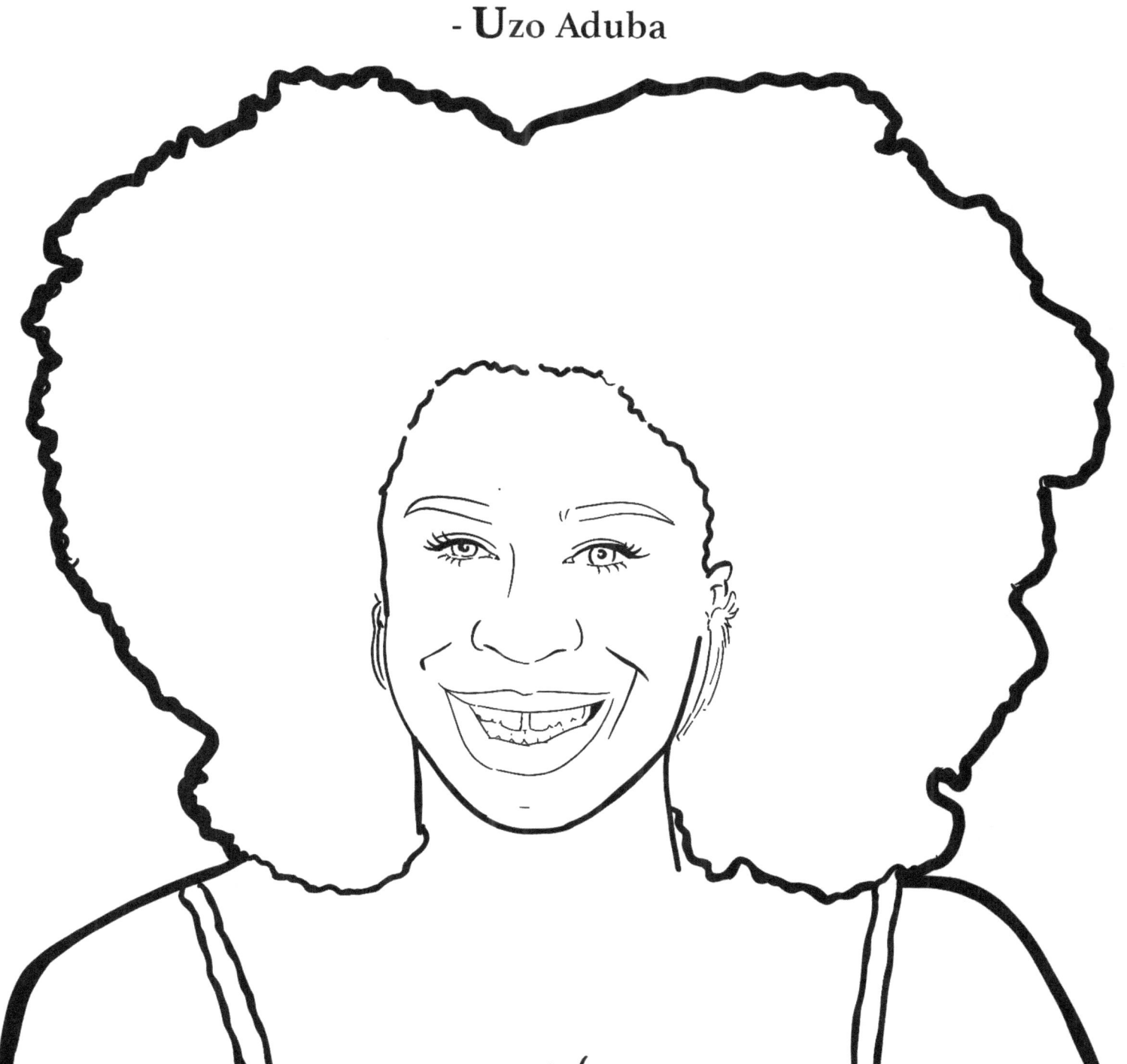

"Do not live someone else's life and someone else's idea of what womanhood is. Womanhood is you. Womanhood is everything that's inside of you."
-Viola Davis

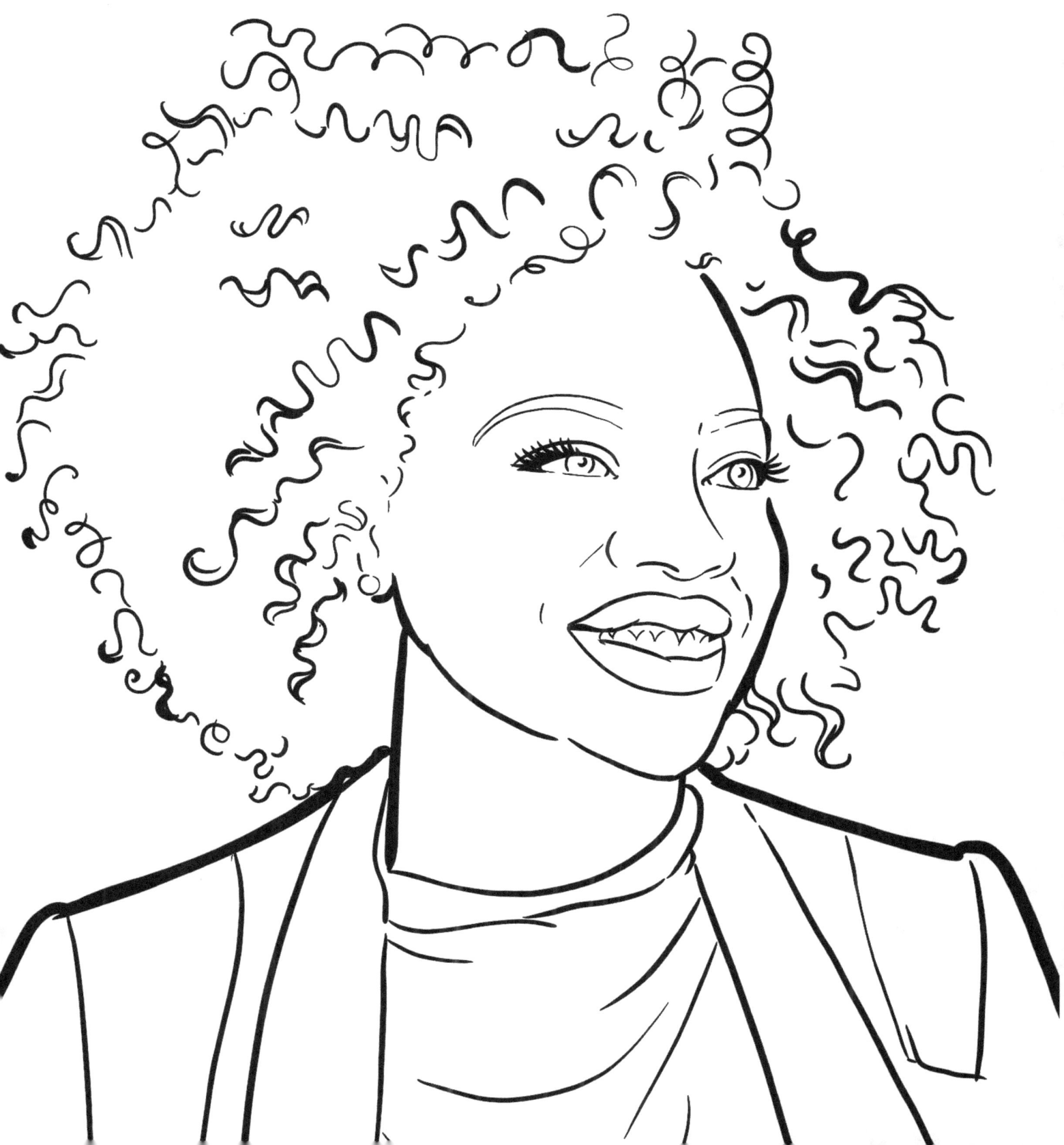

The rage of someone who continues to strive so hard and work so hard but is interrupted every day by society, by racism, by white supremacy, by the patriarchy - how can you not feel empathy?

- **W**unmi Mosaku

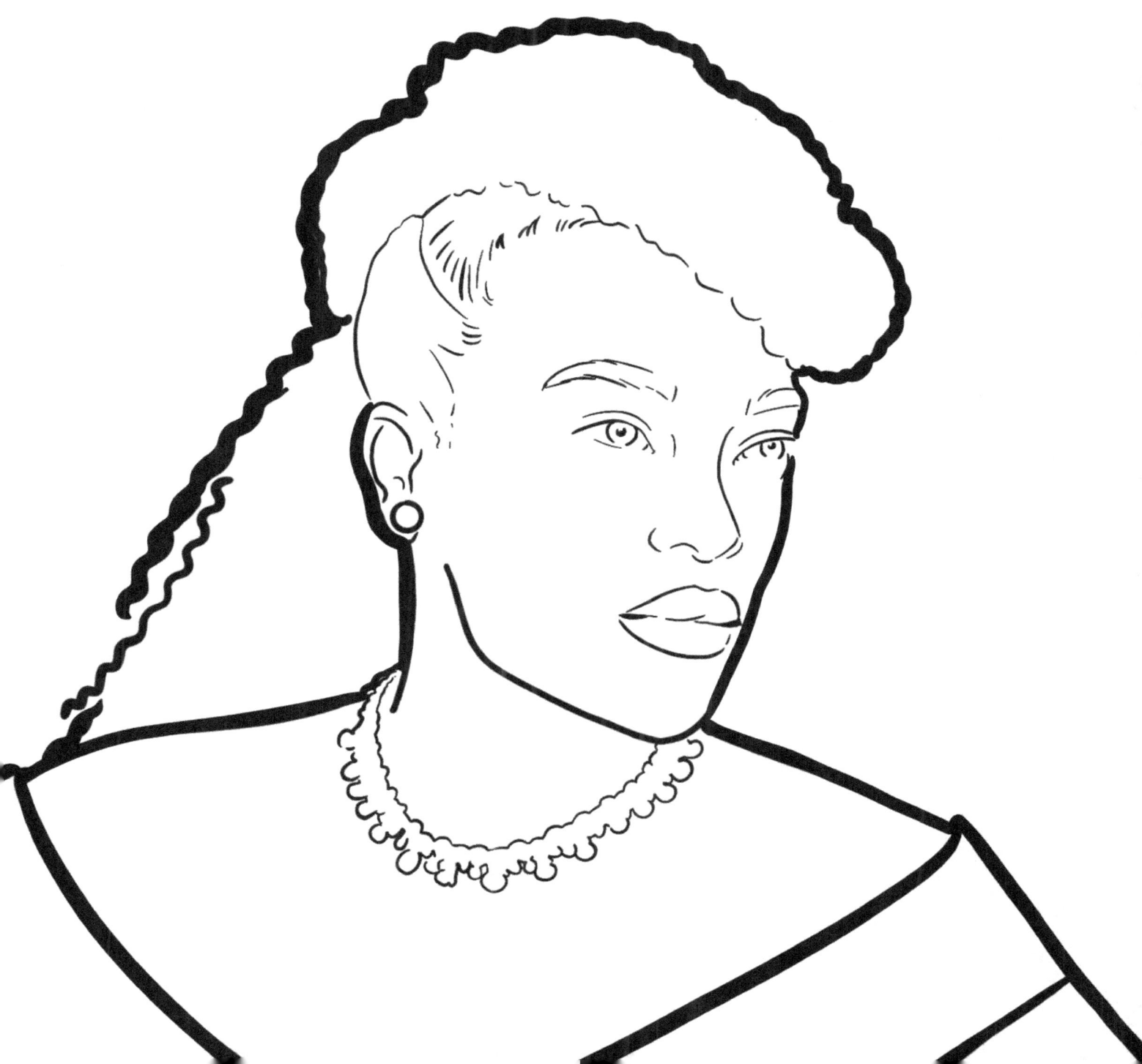

"Never define your success by somebody else's success. I never looked at another man's grass to tell how green mine should be."

- **Xzibit**

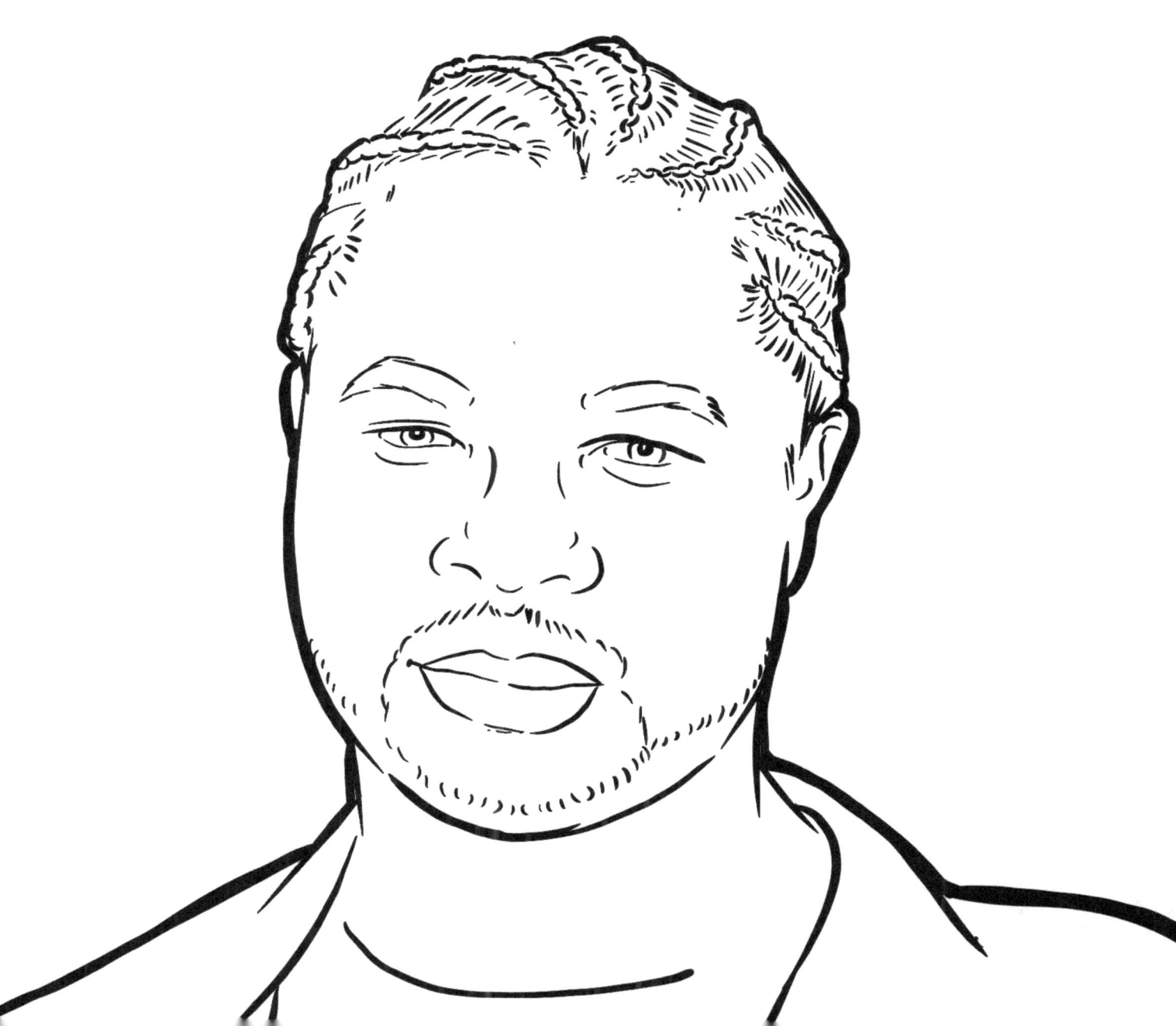

"I don't think I'd be doing the work I'm doing if I wasn't constantly inspired by the other young people doing this work, by the other young people doing work I didn't even realize had to be done. I feel like we constantly educate one another. Because we inherited a world in crisis, we enter this world inspired to make change."

- Yara Shahidi

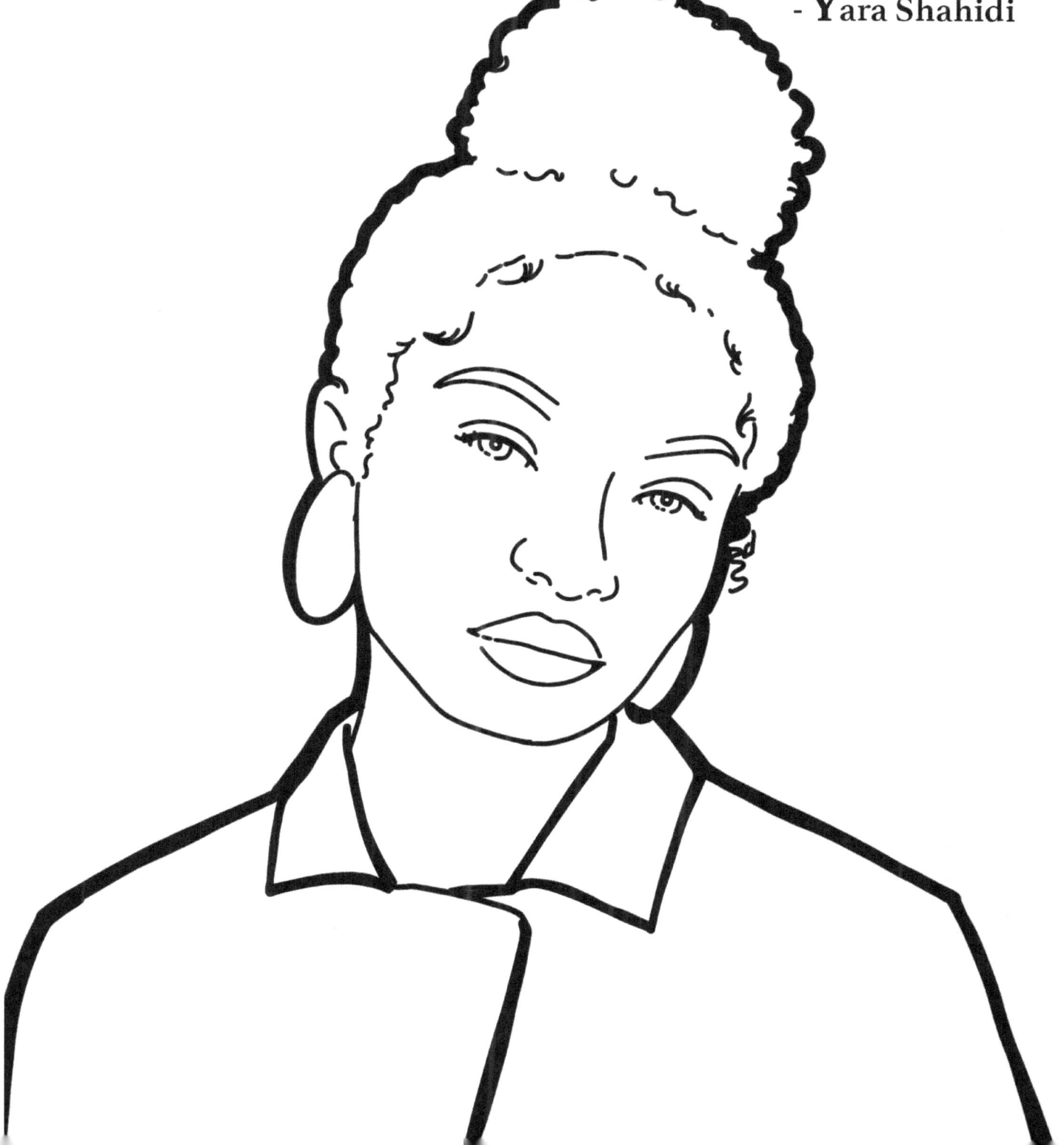

"The best thing is to realize that you are who you are and you gotta work with what you got."

-Zendaya

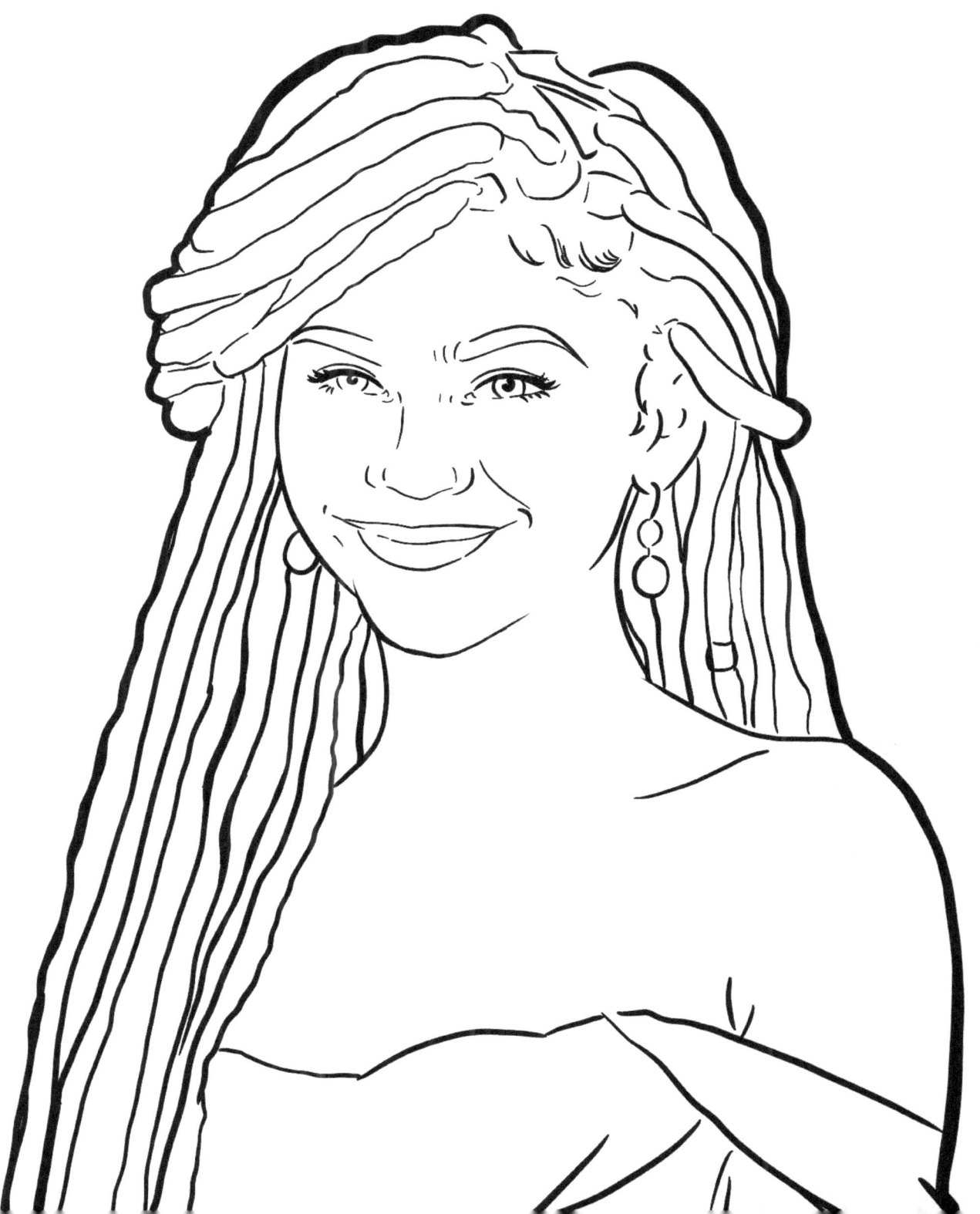

www.ingramcontent.com/pod-product-compliance
Lightning Source LLC
Chambersburg PA
CBHW080908220526
45466CB00011BA/3510